ART FROM FABRIC

with projects using rags, old clothing, and remnants

Gillian Chapman & Pam Robson

Thomson Learning
New York

SALVAGED!

Art from Fabric
Art from Packaging
Art from Paper
Art from Rocks and Shells
Art from Sand and Earth
Art from Wood

First published in the United States in 1995 by
Thomson Learning
New York, NY

Published simultaneously in Great Britain
by Wayland (Publishers) Limited

Library of Congress Cataloging-in-Publication
Chapman, Gillian.
    Art from fabric : with projects using rags, old clothing,
and remnants / Gillian Chapman & Pam Robson.
    p.   cm.—(Salvaged!)
    Includes bibliographical references and index.
    Summary: Provides instructions for using textile remnants
and yarn for making handicraft objects such as fabric collages,
glove puppets, and rag books.
    ISBN 1-56847-381-8
    1. Textile crafts—Juvenile literature. 2. Fabric pictures—
Juvenile literature. [1. Textile crafts. 2. Handicraft.] I. Robson,
Pam. II. Title. III. Series.
NK8804.C53   1995
746—dc20   95-15161

Printed in Italy

Picture Acknowledgments
Ecoscene 4t (Ian Beames);
Eye Ubiquitous 4b (John Hulme); Link 5b (Orde Eliason)
Zefa 5t

*Ninety-five percent of the materials used for the projects
in this book were scraps and remnants.*

Contents

Material Wealth

Fibers and Threads

People have always made use of natural resources for making fabric. Animals like sheep and goats provide hair and fleece for wool. Leather comes from the skin of animals. Silk comes from silkworms. Plants provide fibers, such as cotton and linen, that can be spun and woven into cloth.

To produce new fabric, natural resources are used, either as fabric or for energy to create fabric. Natural resources cannot always be replaced. By reusing rags and cloth remnants you can help conserve the Earth's resources. You can also reduce the growth of local landfills by recycling old garments.

Recycling Fabrics

Poverty forces people to reuse or recycle clothing and remnants. In some developing countries, the most readily available materials are discarded items.

Litter accumulates all over. Four percent of this is old clothing. Much of it can be recycled. Nylon waste, for example, can be made into tennis balls, and old garments can be made into carpet underlay. It is essential that everyone makes the best use of these materials.

People sort garbage at a dump in Bangkok, Thailand, looking for items that can be reused or recycled.

Collecting

For the projects in this book, you can find leftover fabric at tag sales and thrift stores. Look around your home and for old clothing or fabric. Use only clean materials. Remove any buttons or zippers, which can be reused. Woolen items can be unraveled. Small scraps of cloth are useful for collage, appliqué, or patchwork.

Small remnants of fabric can be sewn together to make patchwork quilts. Quilt designs are often traditional.

A scarecrow made from old clothing and fabric remnants. This scarecrow was used to protect crops in a field in southern Africa.

New from Old

Today there is a great demand for crafts made from recycled objects and materials for inspiration. The creativity of the craftspeople depends on the resources available. It is possible to create beauty out of waste.

Quilts known as khols are made from chindi—rags collected and sorted by people in India. In Bangladesh, quilts known as kanthas are made from scraps and the threads of worn-out saris and dhotis. Kanthas are often given as wedding gifts.

In Thailand, scraps of cloth are used to make oven mitts and toys, and silk cocoons are dyed and shaped into flowers. A slipper-sock knitting project in Pakistan employs hundreds of refugees, who use unraveled wool from secondhand knitted garments. Cotton scraps are used to make Indian festival decorations. Cotton rags are used to make paper.

Shifting Shapes

Shape and Size

When you collect discarded fabric and clothing, you might find small decorative items and fasteners, such as buttons, beads, and buckles. Remove them and look at their different shapes. Some will be curved; others will be angular. They will be made from a range of materials—colored plastic for buttons, metal for zippers and fasteners, wood and glass for beads. Sizes will vary from large to tiny, depending upon the garments from which they have been taken.

Discarded fabrics
and trim

Color wheel

Fabric Color Wheel

Look carefully at the items in your collection. You have probably found lots of different fabric remnants—scraps of wool, patches of denim, and pieces of cloth. Trim may include lace, cords, ribbons, tapes, and old shoelaces. Perhaps you have found an odd sock or glove, or feathers from an old hat. You can begin by organizing your collection into a color wheel.

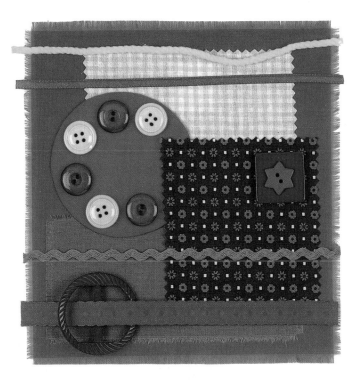

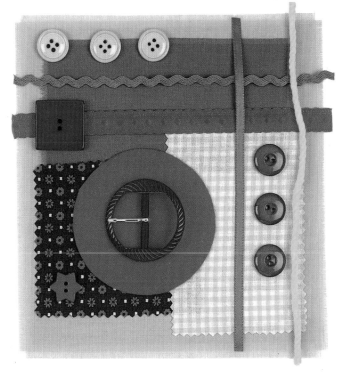

Moving Patterns

Arrange some of the items to create a temporary collage. Move the objects around until you find a pattern you like. You will discover many interesting ways to position the articles.

Shifting Shapes

Make a series of arrangements, using background materials of different colors and textures. Take a photograph, or sketch each one before rearranging them.

Collages (above and left)

7

Fabric Collages

Color and Texture

All fabrics, whether they are natural or manufactured, have special properties. Silk is lightweight and smooth, while wool can be rough. Woven silk fabric is shiny. Woolen cloth has a matte finish and is used to make warm garments. Feel the fabrics in your collection— which are rough and which are smooth? Look at them—which are shiny and which are matte?

Woven or Nonwoven

Most fabrics are woven on a loom, but there are some that are not woven. Felt is made by compression using heat and moisture. A nonwoven fabric will not fray. Fabrics that fray easily can be difficult to use. For a fabric collage, try to choose materials like felt. Some fabrics, such as burlap, are loosely woven, hard, and stiff. Other woven fabrics, such as synthetics like polyester, are soft and delicate.

Underwater collage

Fabric Collage

Make a fabric collage using many colored, textured materials. Plan the design by sketching a picture the same size as the collage you plan to make. Cut your sketch into pieces to use as patterns. Find a large piece of strong fabric or cardboard backing. You can glue your collage to the cardboard or sew the pieces into place onto the strong fabric.

Arrange the collage pieces by following your pattern. If your collage is a landscape or an underwater scene, choose fabrics suited to the subject. Overlap silky materials and netting. Fray and ripple the fabric to create a wavy effect. If you have yarn, trim, and buttons that match your color scheme, use them for details.

You can create an abstract collage by arranging fabric according to color or texture. Put warm or cool colors together or grade them from light to dark.

Color collage (right)

Extra collage materials

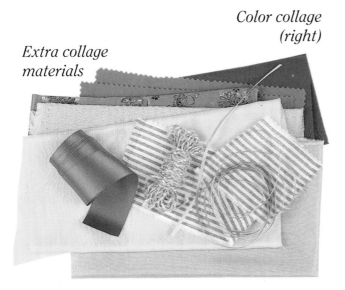

Woven Threads

Spiders' Webs

Spiders are skilled at weaving. The ancient Greek story of Arachne tells how she and the goddess Athena took part in a weaving competition. Arachne was turned into a spider by the jealous Athena because Arachne's weaving was better. Scientists trying to make lightweight fabric strong enough to withstand bullets are experimenting with genetic engineering using the silk genes of spiders.

Warp and Weft

Warp threads lie lengthwise along a roll of cloth. They are the downward threads on a loom. Weft threads are woven in and out across the downward warp threads. Elastic warp threads are best because they must be pulled taut. Threads that do not stretch will snap under tension.

Looms

Weavers work on a frame called a loom. Materials woven on a loom are varied, particularly woolen cloth. Many woolen goods have fluffy surfaces because the fibers lie in different directions. Worsted cloth is smooth because the woolen fibers are combed parallel.

Collecting Threads

Collect threads pulled from a variety of fabrics and materials. See if you can identify them. Are they wool, cotton, linen, or polyester? Are they synthetic or natural? Find a piece of loosely woven fabric, such as burlap. Pull out a number of the weft threads. Weave threads from your collection into the burlap to make a colorful new fabric.

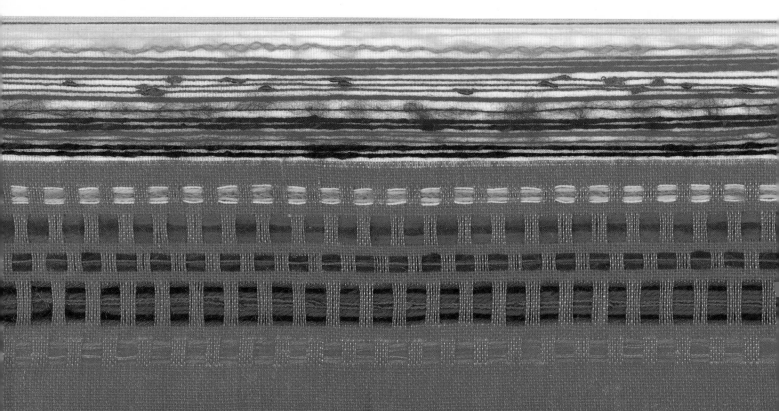

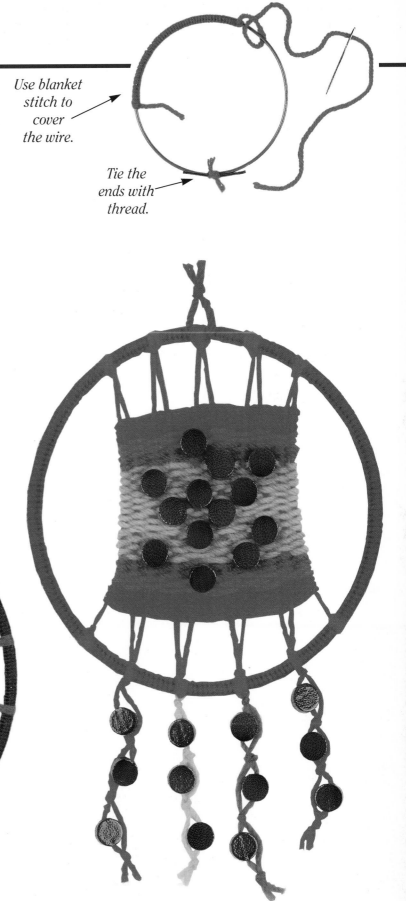

Use blanket stitch to cover the wire.

Tie the ends with thread.

Making a Sunburst

You can make a simple loom by bending a wire coat hanger into a circle. Overlap the ends and tie them with thread. Cover the wire loop with long threads or narrow strips of fabric. Tie threads across the circle and weave other threads in and out, as shown here. Use different textures and thicknesses to create a colorful effect. Decorate the sunburst with trim, such as buttons, beads, and feathers.

Finished sunbursts

Weaving threads (left)

11

Working with Yarn

Weaving Traditions

In Africa, weaving traditions vary considerably. In North Africa, women usually do the weaving. In West Africa and East Africa, it is more likely to be the men. Many different types of looms are used. Today, traditional cloths are being replaced by factory-produced fabrics.

Kente cloth, made by the Asante peoples of Ghana, was once worn only by kings. It is woven from strips of rayon or silk. In Malaysia, songket cloth weaving is an ancient craft. Traditional patterns are woven in gold and silver threads. The finished cloth is worn by Malaysians on ceremonial occasions.

Unraveling hand-knits

Unraveling Yarn

Unwanted knitted garments can easily be recycled. The unraveled yarn is crinkly and this can give interesting texture to your projects. Choose clean hand-knits in good condition. Wind the different yarns onto cardboard bobbins. You can use this yarn for a weaving project.

Making Pom-Poms

Yarns can be used to make colorful pom-poms. To make a pom-pom, cut two cardboard circles the same size. Cut a hole in the center of each circle. Wind the yarn through the two rings until the center hole is full. Cut the wound yarn around the outside edge. Tie strong thread around the center of the yarn alongside the cardboard and knot it tightly. Cut the cardboard rings to remove them.

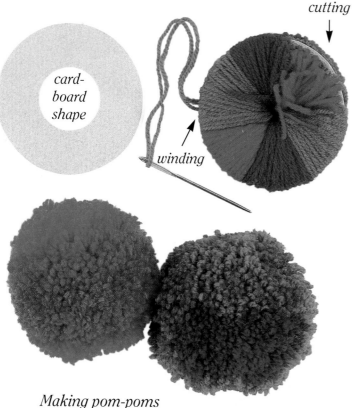

cutting

card-board shape

winding

Making pom-poms

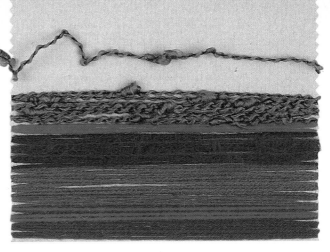

Winding Yarn

In Guatemala, scraps of brightly colored cotton are woven into animalitos—small animals. Here is an idea for winding yarn around pieces of cardboard to make these animal pictures.

Winding wool onto cardboard

You will need a piece of thick cardboard and a selection of yarn. Make small notches in the sides of the cardboard to secure the ends of each length of yarn. Wind the yarn around the cardboard, choosing different colors and textures to create a striped effect.

Find a piece of fabric the same size as the cardboard and cut an animal shape from the center. Place the fabric over the top of the weaving so that the colored stripes show through the animal-shaped hole. Sew or glue the fabric to the cardboard.

Elephant stencil made from fabric

Finished elephant picture

Add fabric features, such as ears.

Decorate the fabric with colored stitching.

Flying Fish

Fishes and Dragons

Wind socks were used by Roman soldiers to find out wind strength and direction for their archers and also to frighten the enemy. In 1066, when the Normans invaded England, the Anglo-Saxon banner was a dragon-shaped wind sock. Historians guessed this because the dragon is on the Bayeux Tapestry.

In Japan, the Boys' Festival is celebrated on the fifth day of the fifth month. Families with boys fly a brightly colored wind sock from the roof. The most popular shape is the carp. This fish struggles to swim upstream each year and symbolizes a boy's journey through life.

Making a carp wind sock

Lightweight Materials

A wind sock must blow easily in the wind and should be made from durable, lightweight material. Synthetic fabric, such as nylon and polyester, has these properties. Old sheets, shirts, and slips are ideal for wind socks.

To make a wind sock, you will need a large piece of fabric, such as a nylon sheet, and smaller scraps of colored material for decoration. The wind sock acts as a wind tunnel, open at both ends. Look at pictures of traditional Japanese windsocks. Use these to sketch a design.

Cutting out the Shape

Follow your design and cut out two body shapes from the fabric. Pin and sew them together.

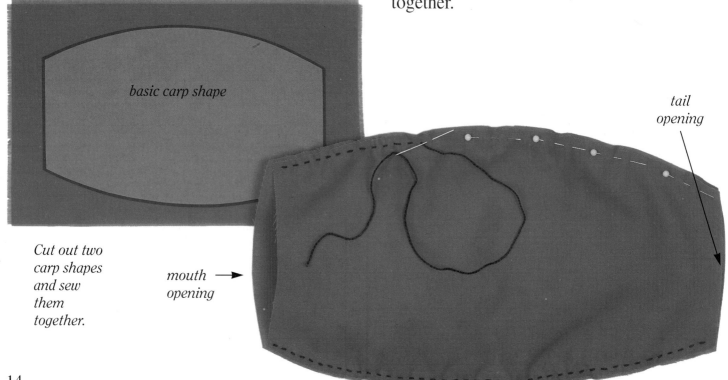

basic carp shape

Cut out two carp shapes and sew them together.

mouth opening →

tail opening

Making a Wind Sock

Make a hem in the mouth opening and thread a length of coat hanger wire through it. Twist the ends of the wire together to make a loop. This will keep the mouth open.

Decorate the wind sock by gluing or sewing pieces of material to the body. Overlap circle shapes for scales, and make pleated fins and a tail.

Tie three lengths of cord to the wire loop and attach these securely to a strong stick. Now find a high, exposed place to attach your wind sock.

coat hanger wire

Sew a hem in opening and thread the wire through.

Making the mouth

Fabric circles and pleats for decoration

Finished carp wind sock

Swooping Snakes

Chinese Kites

Kites existed in China as early as the fifth century B.C. They were flown for pleasure and for military purposes. Kites shaped like mythical birds and dragons were common. Many had rolling eyes and moving tails. Some whistled as they flew and were used to frighten enemies. Kite-flying did not reach Europe until the sixteenth century.

Materials for Kites

A kite must be light and manageable. It must also be strong. The materials to make a kite need to be lightweight and durable. In ancient times, the Chinese used silk or paper for their kites but paper is not durable. Today synthetic fabrics like nylon and polyester can be used.

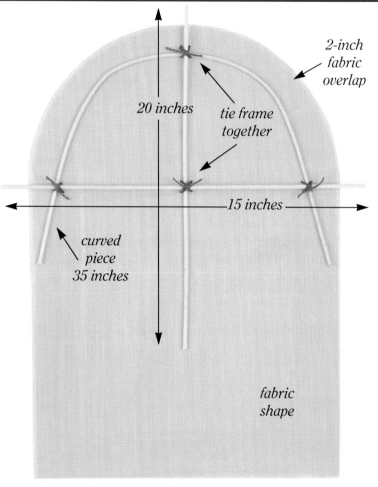

Making the bamboo frame

2-inch fabric overlap

20 inches

tie frame together

15 inches

curved piece 35 inches

fabric shape

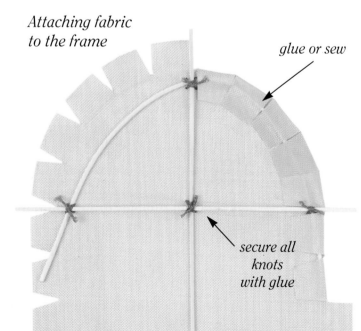

Attaching fabric to the frame

glue or sew

secure all knots with glue

A Snake Kite

This snake kite is easy to make. Because of its flat head and long tail, it can fly in the lightest breeze. Choose lightweight materials to make the kite and decorate it with scraps of colored fabric or paper.

Making the Frame

The frame is made from three pieces of flexible bamboo that are cut to the following sizes: 1 x 20 inches, 1 x 15 inches, and 1 x 35 inches. Assemble the frame by tying the pieces together as shown in the diagram above.

Attaching the Body

Choose a large piece of strong, lightweight fabric for the head. It will need to be larger than the bamboo frame. Place the frame on top of the fabric, as shown opposite. Cut the fabric to the shape of the frame, leaving a two-inch overlap all round. Glue or sew the fabric to the frame. Secure all knots and bindings with blobs of glue to make them extra strong.

Overlap fabric circles for the tail.

Finished snake kite

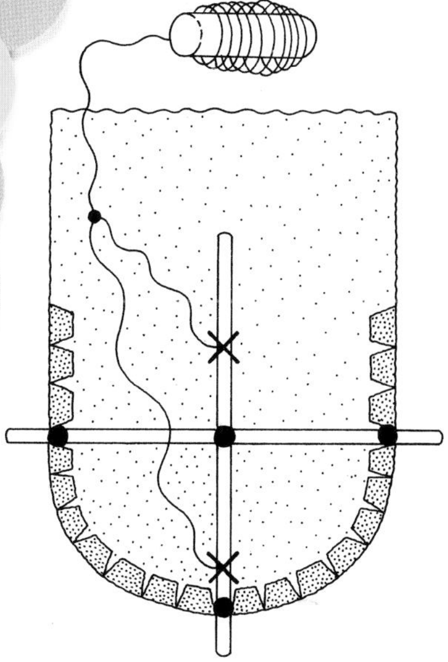

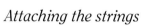

Attaching the strings

Making the Tail

The tail is made from overlapping circles of fabric or paper. Begin by gluing them to the head and attach as many circles as you like.

Rigging the Strings

It is important to make sure the strings are balanced and attached firmly to the kite. Use a strong nylon thread and follow the stringing diagram above.

Be careful when you fly your snake kite. Make sure an adult is nearby and do not stand close to overhead power lines or trees.

Glove Puppets

Traditional Puppets

Puppeteering is an ancient skill common to many cultures. The oldest type of puppeteering began in India, where rod and hand puppet performances were popular forms of entertainment. Hand puppets are simple to make and easy to operate. They are often found in countries that have strong traditions of storytelling and are used to bring a story to life.

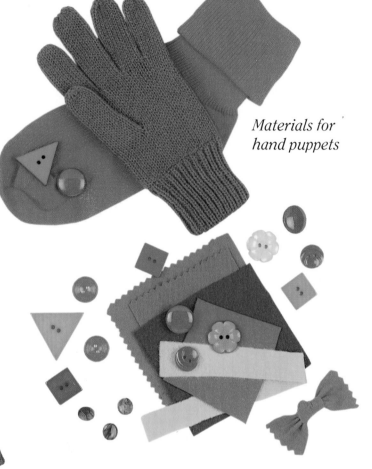

Materials for hand puppets

Marking the position of features

Sewing on features

Making Hand Puppets

If you have socks, mittens, or gloves in your collection of oddments, they can be turned into puppets.

Place your hand inside a sock with your fingers in the toe and thumb in the heel. Push in the sole of the sock and make a fist to form the puppet's mouth. Use a black felt pen to mark where the eyes, nose, and ears should be positioned.

Cut out ears and a tongue from scraps of fabric and sew them into place. Use buttons and beads for the nose and eyes.

Other Ideas

Old gloves and mittens can also be made into puppets. Push in the middle fingers and thumb of an old glove. Stuff the first and little finger with small fabric scraps to make ears for your puppet, then add the other features.

Use old gloves and mittens

Making a Puppet Theater

To make a puppet theater, find a strong cardboard box, large enough for the puppets to move around in. Cut a hole in the front of the box for the stage. Operate the puppets through a smaller hole cut in the back.

Decorating the Theater

Cover the box with material and decorate it with fabric scraps and trim. Make curtains and scenery, attaching them to the inside of the theater. Write a short play for your hand puppets.

Puppet theater

Performing Puppets

Giant Puppets

The largest string puppets originated in Japan. They are called Bunraku and need two or three people to operate them. It takes many years for the operators to master their art. Smaller string puppets are sometimes called marionettes. The strings are attached to a small wooden frame. The puppeteer remains hidden from view while operating the puppets. There may be as many as nine strings on a puppet. It takes skill and practice to operate a string puppet.

Puppet Bodies

A string puppet must have a firm but flexible body. The materials you use must be light but strong. Choose a suitable piece of fabric for the body and attach lengths of yarn or cord. These form the arms and legs. Thread large, heavy buttons to the ends of the strings for hands and feet. For the head, stuff nylon tights with cotton wool or make a woolen pom-pom (see page 12). Sew the head to the fabric body.

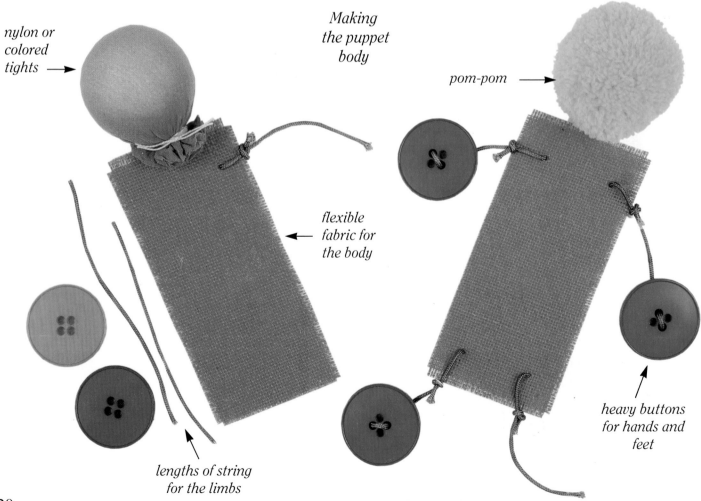

nylon or colored tights →

Making the puppet body

pom-pom →

flexible fabric for the body ←

heavy buttons for hands and feet

lengths of string for the limbs

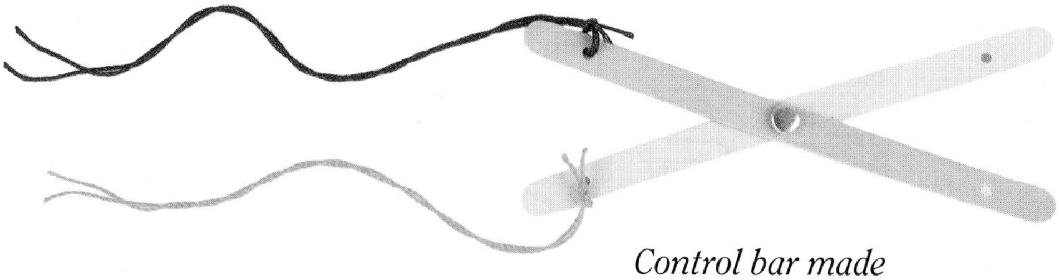

Creating a Character

Once you have made the basic puppet shape, you can decorate it in many ways. Use material to cover the body and limbs, gluing or sewing them together. Be careful not to make the puppet too stiff—it must always move freely. If you have fabric remnants, wool scraps, buttons, and trim, use them imaginatively to create your character.

Control bar made from Popsicle sticks

Attaching the Strings

Use string that is lightweight but strong. The puppet will need strings attached to all four limbs and the head. Thread strings through the button hands and feet and sew one to the top of the head. Make sure you have the correct lengths before trimming the strings. Attach them to a control bar, like the one shown above.

Cat and mouse characters

cat

mouse

21

Rag Rugs

Collecting Rags

In India, particularly in Ahmedabad in Gujarat, women and children collect and sort rags, or chindi, to provide material for the textile industry. The rags are recycled to make items like rag rugs for the local market and for export. Varanasi is well known for its rag rug industry. The rugmakers work mostly in their homes using panja looms.

Rag rugs are based on the common idea of "waste not, want not." Even scraps of fabric that are too small for practical use can be recycled.

Planning a Rag Rug

You will need to collect a large quantity of different fabrics to make a rug. Start by making a smaller mat for practice. Sort the fabrics by type and color and make sure they are all clean. Separate plain and patterned materials and discard any that are too thick. Fine cotton and synthetic fabrics are ideal.

Begin by cutting or tearing the fabrics into long strips. You will be braiding three strips together. The braids will be coiled and sewn together to make the mat. Think about the color scheme of the finished mat. You might use light colors at the center and darker shades around the edge.

Braiding

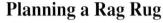

C

B

A

To make a braid, place strip A over the center of strip B. Then place strip C over strip A. Repeat these moves until all the fabric is used.

Different braided effects

Braiding

Lay three lengths of fabric on a flat surface and braid them together, as shown opposite. Use a mixture of colored and patterned fabric to make different effects. Make a number of your braids, until you use up all your fabric.

Coiling and Sewing

The mat is made by coiling the braids into a circular or oval shape and sewing them into place with strong thread. As the braids are wound around, new ones are pinned and sewn in, as shown here. Continue until the mat is the size you want.

Coiling and sewing the braids together

Finished coiled rag rug

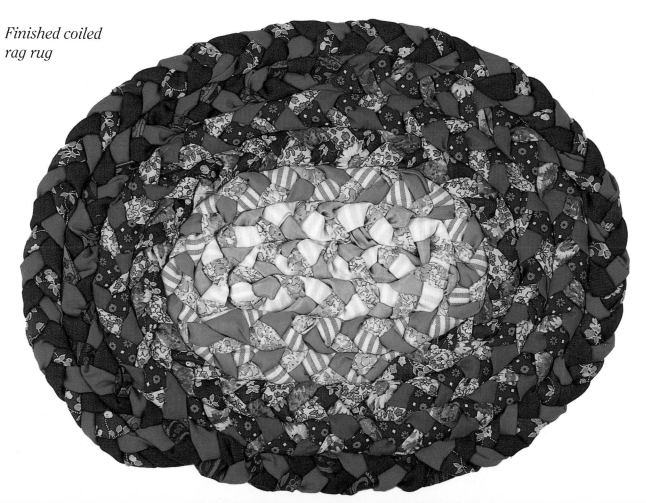

Rag Books

The Meaning of Patchwork

In some societies the use of discarded items to create something whole has a religious significance. Hindus and Buddhists see the patching of cloth as an act of humility. Raffia dance skirts worn by the Kuba women of Africa were often patched. These comma-shaped patches were then turned into a design known as "shina mboa"—the tail of the dog. In the United States, patchwork patterns are given names, such as the Ohio Star. Amish quilts have striking abstract designs.

A Picture of the Past

Articles of clothing can remind us of people and past events. You may look at an old item of clothing and remember the occasion on which it was worn. It might have been a wedding or a birthday party. Gather scraps of fabric from such garments and piece them together to create a patchwork history of your family. Design a picture in the form of a family tree. Choose suitable material and make a patch for each member of the family.

Patchwork family tree

youngest generation at the top

A Patchwork Story

You can make a patchwork storybook from your collection. Use pieces of household fabrics, such as old curtain or upholstery material, to make the pages of the book. Sew them together using a running stitch. Choose fabrics that remind you of a particular house or room.

Collect scraps of fabric from old clothing belonging to your family. Some scraps may have special memories and stories attached to them. Make patch pockets from these pieces of fabric and sew them into the book. Write about the fabrics and the people associated with them and put the stories, with any photographs, inside.

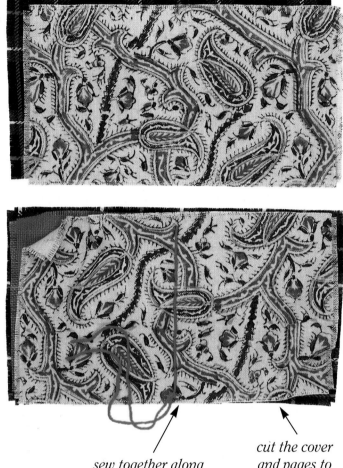

sew together along the center fold

cut the cover and pages to the same size

Making a book from fabric

label for the title

pockets containing stories and photographs

My Family

My Home

New Clothes from Old

Fashionable Clothes

The fashion world is becoming more conscious of the environment. Some designers are choosing fibers like cotton only if they have been grown without the use of pesticides. The finished clothes are expensive, but changes are coming. Tencel is a new fabric that is a mixture of wood pulp and cotton.

Patchwork hat

Patching to create a new fabric

Fashionable Patching

Hard times make it necessary to patch and mend clothes. Nowadays, it is even common practice to patch the elbows and knees on new garments to prevent wear and tear. Sometimes patchwork is used on clothes and bags because it is fashionable.

Look through your collection of materials and make a new fabric by sewing pieces together. Design and make something useful. Keep your ideas simple and make paper patterns first as references.

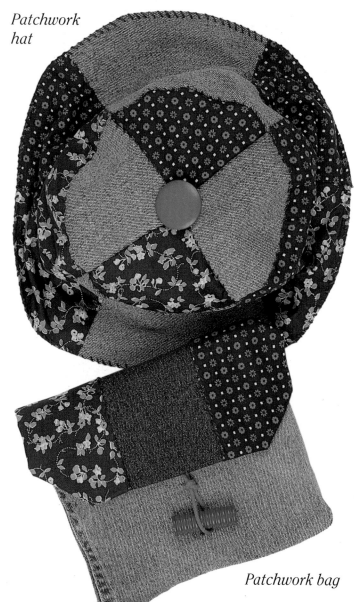

Patchwork bag

Weaving Ties

New and exciting fabrics can be made by weaving old, unwanted items together. Ties quickly become unfashionable and are discarded. Collect together as many colorful and silky discarded ties as you can find. Weave them together to make new fabric.

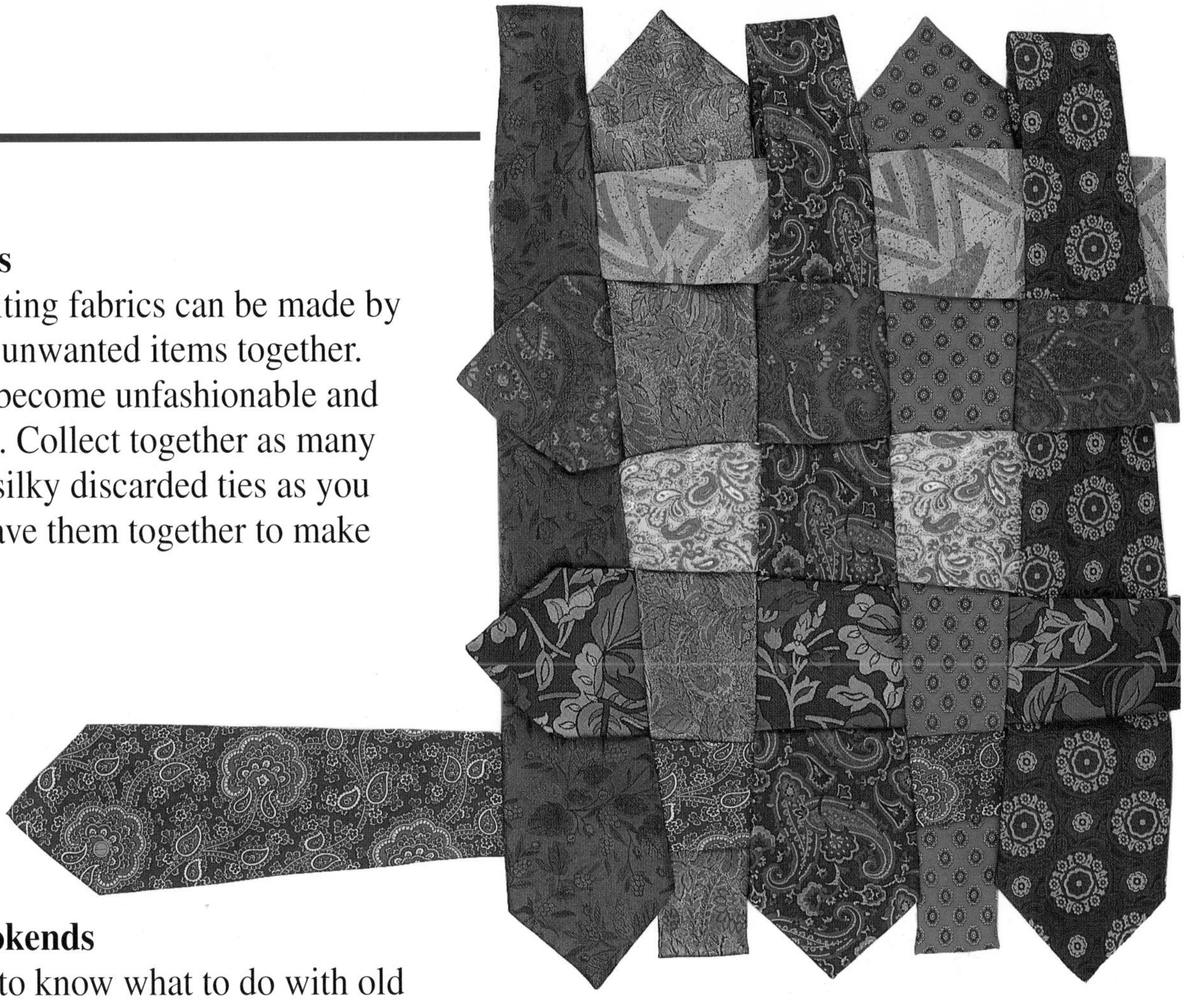

Weaving old ties

Sneaker Bookends

It is difficult to know what to do with old sneakers that are worn out or too small. Wash them and then try painting them with acrylic paints. Fill them with stones or plaster to make them heavy and use them as bookends.

Sneaker bookends

Rag Dolls

Ancient Dolls

Examples of the first rag dolls can be seen in museums today. One doll found in Egypt was made from coarse fabric and stuffed with rags.

Rag Dolls

In some places, children play with toys that they have made at home. Their families are too poor to buy toys, so they make toys from discarded materials. Some of these toys are very intricate. They vary from models of helicopters to simple rag dolls.

Making a Rag Doll

This rag doll is made from scraps of colored fabric and wool. Make the head by cutting the foot off a pair of nylon tights. Stuff it with cotton or rags to make a ball shape. Cover the ball with a length of fabric, tying it tightly at the neck with yarn.

Roll up another length of fabric to make an arm shape, binding it with yarn at each end to form hands. Divide the fabric at the neck and tie the arms into place around the waist. This makes the basic doll shape. Tuck extra fabric strips into the waist band.

Making the doll

making the head

attaching the arms

dressing the doll

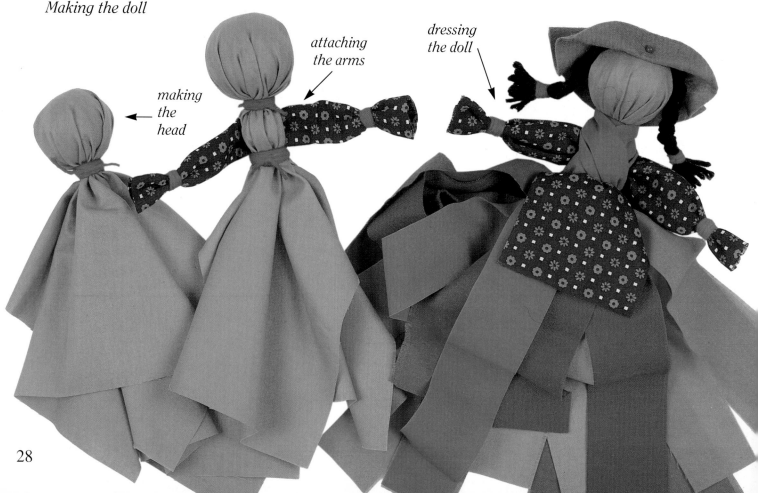

Worry Dolls

Children of Central America traditionally tell their troubles and worries to tiny dolls before going to sleep at night. These dolls are made from colored threads. There is one doll for each worry. The dolls are placed under the pillows of the children, who believe that while they are asleep the dolls will solve all their problems.

Making a pipe cleaner body

Make a family of worry dolls and keep them in a drawstring bag

Making Worry Dolls

You can make your own worry dolls and tell your troubles to them. Make the bodies from pipe cleaners, twisting them into shape as shown here. Wrap yarn around the pipe cleaners, using different colors for the features and clothes. Make a complete family and keep them in a little bag.

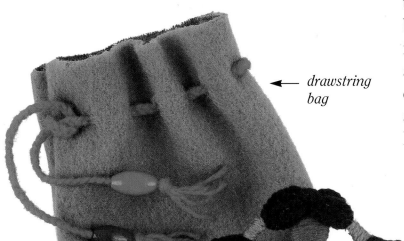

← *drawstring bag*

Glossary

Bayeux Tapestry An embroidery, 231 feet long and 20 inches wide, that tells the story of the Norman invasion of England in 1066.

Bunraku Style of puppetry that originated in the sixteenth century in Japan. The large string puppets need three puppeteers to operate them.

burlap A coarse jute fabric often used to make sacks.

chindi Rags sorted into bundles by Hindu women and children, mainly in Ahmedabad in Gujarat in India. The rags are recycled in textile mills.

durable Able to last for a long time.

fabric Any cloth, woven or nonwoven, made from yarn or fibers.

fibers Natural or synthetic filaments that can be spun into yarn.

flexible Able to bend easily without breaking.

garments Articles of clothing.

genetic engineering When humans alter nature by constructing and combining genes.

hem A folded edge on a piece of cloth, usually stitched down.

knitting A way of looping and entwining yarn with long eyeless needles to make cloth.

loom A frame on which yarn is woven into cloth.

marionettes Puppets with jointed limbs worked by strings.

material Substance from which something is made.

oddment Something leftover; a remnant.

panja looms Devices found in Indian homes and used to weave rag rugs.

remnant A piece of left-over fabric.

synthetic Manmade material.

taut Tightly stretched.

Tencel A new textile made from wood pulp and cotton.

threads Strands of material, usually fabric.

warp The lengthwise fixed threads on a loom.

weft Threads woven in and out across the lengthwise warp threads on a loom.

worsted Woolen fabric with a hard, smooth, close-textured surface.

yarn A continuous strand of fibers used in weaving and knitting.

More Information

Further Reading

Bawden, Juliet. *Fun with Fabric*. New York: Random House Books for Young Readers, 1993.

James, Barbara. *Waste and Recycling*. Conserving Our World. Milwaukee: Raintree Steck-Vaughn, 1990.

Javna, John. *Fifty Simple Things Kids Can Do to Save the Earth*. Kansas City, MO: Andrews & McMeel, 1990.

Lancaster, John. *Fabric Art*. Fresh Start. New York: Franklin Watts, 1991.

Morley, Jacqueline. *Clothes: For Work, Play & Display*. Timelines. New York: Franklin Watts, 1992.

O'Reilly, Suzie. *Knitting and Crochet*. Arts & Crafts. New York: Thomson Learning, 1994.

O'Reilly, Suzie. *Weaving*. Arts & Crafts. New York: Thomson Learning, 1993.

Stocks, Sue. *Collage*. First Arts and Crafts. New York: Thomson Learning, 1994.

Sources for Special Materials

Thrift stores, tag sales, and the remnant sections of fabric and craft stores are all good places to find fabric for the crafts in this book.

Addresses for Information

Center for Marine Conservation
1725 Desales Street NW, Suite 500
Washington, DC 20036

Environmental Protection Agency
Public Information Center
Washington, DC 20460

Environmental Defense Fund
257 Park Avenue South
New York, NY 10010

Friends of the Earth
218 D Street SE
Washington, DC 20003

Greenpeace
1436 U Street NW
Washington, DC 20009

National Wildlife Federation
1400 16th Street NW
Washington, DC 20036

The Nature Conservancy
1436 North Lynn Street
Arlington, VA 22209

Rainforest Action Network
300 Broadway, Suite 28
San Francisco, CA 94133

Index